CREATING A LOCAL HISTORICAL BOOK:

FICTION AND NON-FICTION GENRES

TYLER R. TICHELAAR

Modern History Press

Cover photo: "Ridge and Blaker Streets, Marquette, MI circa 1910."
Courtesy of Jack Deo, Superior View.

ISBN-13 978-1-61599-178-5 (paperback)
ISBN-13 978-1-61599-179-2 (eBook)

Modern History Press
5145 Pontiac Trail
Ann Arbor, MI 48105
www.ModernHistoryPress.com
info@ModernHistoryPress.com

Fax 734-663-6861
Tollfree USA/CAN 888-761-6268
London, England: 44-20-331-81304

Contents

List of Pictures in this Book

Creating a Local Historical Book

The following article is based on a transcript of the February 2011 interview of Tyler R. Tichelaar on Authors Access podcast with hosts Victor R. Volkman and Irene Watson. Due to the intense public response to this broadcast, we have made it available in this form for your enjoyment. You can still listen to the original recording by visiting the archive page at

http://www.authorsaccess.com/category/genres/historical-books

Legend: Tyler Tichelaar (TT); Victor Volkman (VV); Irene Watson (IW)

IW: Good evening, ladies and gentlemen, and welcome to Authors Access, where authors get published and published authors get successful. Hi, I am Irene Watson and I am the managing editor of Reader Views.

VV: And I am Victor Volkman from Loving Healing Press in Ann Arbor, Michigan. I would like to welcome all our listeners to episode number 129 in our series. Tonight's topic will be *Creating a Local Historical Book* with special guest Tyler Tichelaar. You can learn more about our guest on the Authors Access website, which is: authorsaccess.com.

Tonight we are on the line with Tyler R. Tichelaar, a seventh generation Marquette, Michigan resident, who has written five novels with many more to come, all set in Upper Michigan, including: *The Marquette Trilogy*, the award-winning *Narrow Lives*, and the most recently published, a history of Marquette entitled *My Marquette: Explore the Queen City of the North, Its History, People, and Places.*

Tyler has a PhD in Literature from Western Michigan University and Bachelor and Master's degrees from Northern Michigan University. He has lectured in Writing and Literature at Clemson University, the University of Wisconsin, and the University of London. Tyler is also a regular guest-host on our show—which you know—and the President of the Upper Peninsula Publishers and Authors Association. He is the owner of Marquette Fiction and Superior Book Promotions—a professional book review and editing and proofreading service. Besides writing about Upper Michigan, he is interested in the Arthurian legends, and recently published *King Arthur's Children*, a study of treatments of King Arthur's children in literature from medieval times to twenty-first century novels. Tyler currently lives in Marquette, Michigan, where the roar of Lake Superior, mountains of snow, and sandstone architecture continue to inspire his writing. Good evening, Tyler!

TT: Hi, Victor and Irene, it's great to be here. It is different being on the other side, not being the host.

IW: *[laugh]*. Yes, I can well imagine this, and this is really interesting to be talking to you. You are a very diverse writer, from fiction to all of a sudden the *My Marquette* that you wrote, which is non-fiction. Although it is historical as your other three books were—*The Marquette Trilogy*—but this is really different because it is not fiction. Let me start off immediately just talking about what kind of different types of research did you have to do in comparison to doing the fiction, which was historical, to the non-fiction?

TT: OK, sure. In writing, a lot of it overlapped, and in writing the novels, I basically did almost all the research. I would say probably about 80 percent or so of the research into *My Marquette* also was used in my novels. The main difference, I think, is I did not have to be as specific in the novels; I did not have to pin down specific dates; I usually could link things, and just as long as I got the year, an event took place, that was close enough. Whereas with writing the non-fiction book, the thing that frustrated me the most was trying to pin down a specific date. I would read one source that would say, this happened on February 28th, and the next source would say February 25th, and the third source would say February 27th. I would have to dig back and figure out what their sources were and maybe look up the actual newspapers that covered the event back in the day. I would sometimes spend hours just trying to check one little date, just to make sure that it would be accurate. That took a lot of time and because I was writing about real people—the actual historical people—I needed to do a lot more research into their backgrounds, especially since a whole section of my book is about historical homes in the area. There have been other Marquette history books, but none of them covered the historical residential district as thoroughly as mine has, and for me, that was the really exciting part of the book because I had always been fascinated by all these old Victorian homes and who would have lived in them.

In researching them, I discovered that almost everybody, who lived on those couple of streets in Marquette, were all related to each other in some way—either through blood or through marriage. So I spent all this time trying to sort out those family trees, to keep track of them. Then I made a genealogy chart, so people reading the book could follow who was who in the story, which was not something that I needed to do in my novels—the historical people just made cameo appearances as I referred to somebody. Basically, I guess for the non-fiction books, a lot more time was spent ironing out the little details.

IW: So, you were writing novels. Why did you decide to write a local history book?

TT: Well, I really was never interested in writing a history book, partly because it seemed sort of an overwhelming task to do. And there had already been a couple of history books written about the area in the past. I initially wanted to write novels just because I thought that the area deserved to be treated on a higher level. The significance of it through all of American history needed to be made apparent, and I felt like the American Dream was really played out right here in Upper Michigan. And I kind of wanted to memorialize that and honor that in

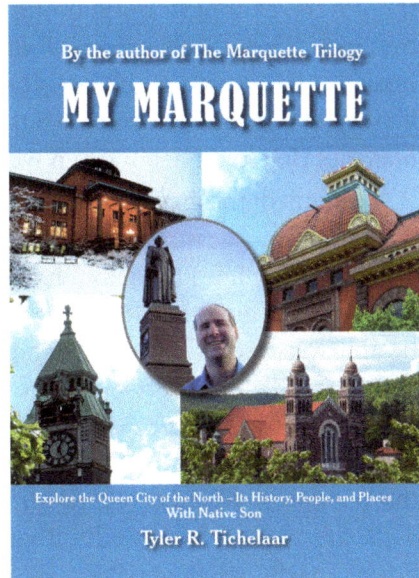

my novels. I thought I was doing something that was very unique for the area. The novels sold well enough, but the bookstores—when I brought the novels to them—they said, "What we really need is a history of Marquette; that's what the tourists are asking for," and the histories that had been written were basically out of print at that point.

I hemmed and hawed about it; I did not really want to do it. I had thought about writing a book explaining all sorts of my thoughts and the reasons behind the way I had written the novels. And people were asking me to give them tours of the city. I thought, not everybody will be able to come to Marquette and have me give him a walking tour, so maybe it would be better if I wrote a book that was laid out as a tour book. And so *My Marquette*, the history book, ended up being laid out like a tour book. Rather than telling the whole story chronologically, the book logically takes readers from place to place, so that you could walk around, and I would tell you the history of the building, or the house, park, whatever the case was. Once I did that, I felt more comfortable with it and I wanted to personalize it too, and say not just, "These are the events that happened," but "This is why this place matters to me." So I made it very personal, I talked about growing up in the area, I talked about things that my family had done: my grandpa building the post office, my ancestors—they helped to build up the Methodist Church, different things along those lines.

What I think was probably my smartest move is I did some cross-selling in the book. I had quotes from all of my novels in the book for different places. For example, Doncker's Candy Store that I mentioned, I would quote the passage from one of the novels where the characters go to Doncker's. Same thing with the library, I write about the library, but I have the quote from one of my books about the characters at the library. So hopefully that would encourage people also to read my novels.

VV: Great, that is a unique approach of bringing a sense of place to history which can be hard nowadays to keep it consistent—the interest level, and this way people can browse. What are some other ways that your book is different from other typical local histories?

TT: The fact that *My Marquette* is laid out as a walking tour makes it very user-friendly. I put a lot of maps in the book, broken up by the different sections, so you do not just have a map of Marquette; you have a map specifically of the downtown, of the residential section, or the harbor. Also, because I included a lot of genealogies of different families in Marquette history, that helps a lot with understanding the different families and the reasons they came here, which has mostly to do with the discovery of iron ore here, and also of the logging industry and a lot of the shipping that went on in the area. I included my own family trees, and fortunately for me, my family—part of the reason why I'm so interested in Marquette's history is that my family has been here since the town was founded in 1849, so I could connect myself to events that happened in a lot of places, to great-grandparents, great-great-grandparents.

The other thing is, a lot of books have lots of historical photos. I think that historical photos really, really, brought it to life and I tried to make a real effort to have pictures be very large and have pictures for every single section. A lot of history books tend to focus on just the past—the distant past—but I tried to have photos of current buildings and photos of buildings that are not there anymore, but were there within recent memory. The buildings that were there in the '80s and the '90s; even when I went to the historical society—anything that happened in Marquette after about 1950—they did not have much information on. It is because it was not really considered that historical yet at that point, so people did not preserve it. I tried to do as much as I could to work well on that, so that it would be a book that would be of interest to people who were alive now, who can remember a lot of the places and events that happened.

VV: Great. Given that you have such a huge scope of 150 years, and a couple of square miles, where do you draw the line about what is in bounds and what is out of bounds?

TT: That was a really difficult thing for me to do. What it basically came down to was, had those places already been mentioned in my novels, so that I could have quotes for each section, so I would have consistency. There are one or two exceptions in the book where I did not mention—on the places I mentioned in my book—in one of my novels before, but for the most part I did. Whether or not I felt I had something to say about the place and its significance to me, there were several places that I thought, "Well, this place is important, I should include it, but what do I really have to say about it that has not been said before?" So I did not necessarily mention those.

I do not think I missed too many places that people would consider major. I had one guy come up to me at a book signing and say, "Well, you did not include my high school in there. Shame on you!" and I *[laugh]*—I just—it never crossed my mind to include that school in the book, which is funny, because it is the school that my grandma graduated from. I should have thought of that, but I could not include everything; there is no way. The book was supposed to end up being about 250-300 pages, and it ended up being 448 pages. So there is no way that I could include everything. But I tried to divide the city up into sections and then tried to digest each section by mentioning what I thought were the highlights of the major places, as well as drawing in some interesting facts that I did not think most people would know.

IW: This is quite an undertaking job you took, Tyler. What is the population of Marquette?

TT: It is about 20,000.

IW: OK. Obviously, it is a fair-sized city. There are a lot of steps—historical steps—that you had to research on; what was the most difficult part for you in this whole process?

TT: I would have to say probably—and it sounds awful *[laugh]*—but probably for me, having not written a history book before, I felt like my role largely was just cutting and pasting things. I would research books—other history books—from the past and I had all these clippings from magazines and newspapers and information and I felt all I did was to gather information and put it together. I found myself kind of bored actually, just doing that. It was not creative, like in writing a novel. And I always felt, that I had—hanging over my shoulder—the people who were going to say, "Oh, you got that date wrong," or, "That event, that detail is not accurate," or something like that. So, double-checking all of those facts and making sure that they are correct was probably the most difficult part.

IW: But it must have been very rewarding in the end for you?

TT: Yes, I am very proud of the book. I am especially proud of how it looks. It ended up looking the way I imagined it to be, plus even better than that, and I think that helps a lot. The colors on the cover, and the layout of the book, of the photographs, and how they were laid out. I decided to make it quite large, 8.5 x 11; I wanted it to be a kind of coffee-table sort of a book. It really has resonated with people, they have given positive responses. I have gotten letters from people and wonderful responses that really have made it all worthwhile in the end.

IW: I am sure it does. You use photographs; obviously you have to get a lot of permission to use a lot of them. What process did you have to go through to attain some of these photographs and actually be able to use them, or have permission to use them?

TT: Well, the photographs came from several different sources. First, a fellow local author, Sonny Longtine, who had previously written the book *Marquette, Then and Now*, which was out-of-print. People had been badgering him for years to reprint the book and he just did not want to do it, for whatever reason. I did not want to step on his toes by coming out with my book, so I talked to him about it. He said, "Oh, no, go ahead and write it and I have got all these photos from my book if you want to use them." He gave me several photos, most of them were photos that I could have taken myself, but there were some pictures of things, for example, the railroad trestle that used to be downtown; he had a picture of it when they took it down back in perhaps 1999 or 2000. I could never have taken a picture of it any longer, so he was a great resource that way and very generous about sharing his pictures.

Obvious places to get photos were the Historical Museum here in Marquette; I got lots of pictures from them. Also from Superior View, which is owned by Jack Deo. He has been a collector of old photographs for decades and has collections of people who were photographers in the Marquette area back in the 1800s. He has this huge collection of photographs and I got several from him.

In one case, I had to write to the Utah Historical Society for a picture of my great-great-grandpa's cousin because he happened to have moved out there and that was a certain place that I could find a photo of him.

The most frustrating part for me was not being able to get photos that I wanted. I was lucky, actually, in the end. The Marquette Mall used to have this wonderful fountain in it and I could not find a picture of this fountain. It had these colored lights in the water and the water would shoot up, so there were pink and green sprays of water. It was a gorgeous fountain; everybody loved it. It was a shame when they took it out. I could not find a picture of that fountain, and finally I went to the historical society. I was looking for something completely different

Railroad trestle removal in downtown Marquette (1999-2000)
Photo Credit: Sonny Longtine

Former Marquette County History Museum where Tyler did his research

and I happened to find a picture of the fountain. It was not at all a picture that was what I was expecting; it actually showed a bunch of Boy Scouts in a canoe in the fountain doing some sort of an exhibition. It was a kind of bizarre picture, but at least I got my picture of my fountain.

Another thing I wanted was a picture of the Bavarian Inn that had been torn down; nobody had one. I checked at the museums and the university archives, and it ended up my great-aunt had a photo of it. I wanted it specifically because my grandpa and my great-uncle had helped to build it. We had to dig through my great-uncle's photographs which took a couple of hours before we finally found the picture.

Marquette is well-known for having been the site of the filming of the movie *Anatomy of a Murder* (1959). It was based on Robert Traver's 1958 book about a murder that took place here. When they filmed the movie, all the Hollywood movie stars came to the area and they actually filmed it here: Jimmy Stewart, Lee Remick, Ben Gazzara, a whole bunch of stars from back in the '50s. I wanted a couple of pictures of when the movie stars were here. I went to the Northern Michigan University archive and they had photos, but they said, even if these photos were in the collection, they could not grant permission

Bavarian Inn - another local landmark which has disappeared

to me to use them. They said I would have to write to whoever actually took the photos. The photos were taken by *Look* magazine, which hasn't been published since 1971. I did some research on the Internet and—as far as I could tell—it seemed like all of the materials were now in the Library of Congress. So if I wanted to use those photos, I would have to write to the Library of Congress for permission. I was not really clear if the photos were in the public domain just because they were in the collection.

I was kind of irritated about all that process trying to get those. Then I talked to the woman who owned Globe Printing—Stacey Willey. Globe Printing did the printing of my book, and their office is above the Roosevelt Bar, which is where all the movie stars signed their names on the wall when they were here. She had—because their office is in that building—people always coming in there to see this wall with Jimmy Stewart's handwriting on it. And people have been giving her photos over the years that they took when this movie was filmed. She had some pictures that were taken by locals and she let me use those. So I kind of got around the whole permission-seeking that way. Those are just some ideas of different avenues I had to go down to find the photos.

VV: Yep. I think your experience was probably pretty common; our local historians have to be pretty ingenious to get what they want. Let's shift gears a little bit and talk about marketing. Have you done just the conventional route of museums and gift shops? Please give us a whole idea of what you have done?

TT: Yes, conventional in the sense that I brought the books down to all the bookstores, the museums, the gift shops, places where my other books were already for sale. Those were all very helpful to that extent. I actually started blogging for the first time; I had always been resistant about it, but I decided I would have a blog and posted segments from the book on the blog. I do not always post all the photos from the book, but I always put that "There were photos of these things in the book," hopefully encouraging people reading the blog to then buy the book. I advertise the blog on Facebook and Myspace and so forth.

With this book I was a lot more successful; people apparently like history more than they like novels. I had a lot more success with getting media coverage for this book. I had a book signing at Snowbound Books and the local television station just showed up and filmed me signing books. I managed to get the local paper—*The Mining Journal*—to do a feature story, so that was on the front page of the paper. That generated quite a few sales; in fact I was out of town that weekend and the bookstores all left me a bunch of messages, saying, "We are out of your books..."

VV: Wow...

TT: I had to run in and deliver the books the day after. The story came out on a Sunday, so I got home on Monday and had to deliver a bunch of books. I went to the craft shows at Christmas, I had stuff going on every weekend in pretty much November and December, you know, gearing up toward the holidays. I was lucky enough to be on *The Doug Garrison Show* here, which is a local show to promote the area, the arts and local things of interest. That program just started up this fall, so I was one of the first guests on there. I had people just calling me up and asking me to come and do events. I got called about a week ago to come and speak to the Northern Center for Lifelong Learning to talk to them in April 2012. I got a call a couple of days ago to come and speak to a library group in Iron River which is about a couple of hours away, which it kind of surprised me that they were interested. I got an order from the Iron Mountain Library about eighty miles away; they wanted three copies of the book. Lots more publicity from a history book than I ever experienced with my novels. It is kind of a surprise to me that it has been as popular as it has been.

VV: Well, that is really a great story to get that kind of recognition, and I am sure that feels really good. What kind of advice do you have for authors just starting out in local history?

TT: Do you mean in terms of writing a book?

VV: Well, let us suppose they have a great idea for doing some part of a city, county, or historical district that they feel has been under-served or perhaps there has not been a new local history book out in twenty years, and they feel inspired, but they are not really sure how to get going?

TT: I would say, do your research and try to find whatever has been written, whether it is a history book that was written many years ago, that you could use as a starting point. Or local museums and see what you can find. Look through rolls of microfilms and old newspapers, whatever you can do along those lines. As you work through it, you try to decide what you are going to include, and eventually a structure comes out of that. You decide whether your book has to be divided up into sections—twenty-year periods, fifty-year periods—along those lines. And talk to as many people as possible, especially older people, even people at museums, libraries. Do not be afraid of telling the people that you want to write a book about the area, because people get excited about it. I had lots of people wanting to share information with me, more information than I possibly could have used.

I would go down to the museum here and I would say, "I am looking for this one specific fact," and the research librarian there—she was wonderful. She had all kinds of ideas, of ways, which you can go about finding information. I was very focused and just wanted to find this one thing, but she would say, "Well, here are all these other possibilities." I ended up looking at all these other files and finding new information and I ended up corresponding with family members, like grandchildren, great-grandchildren of people who were significant to Marquette one hundred years ago and now very much wanted to share family stories. I had people look at the genealogy charts I made, just to make sure I did not make any mistakes there. I feel that especially if you are just getting started and it is an area that has been under-served, I would say, talk to as many people as possible and all kinds of materials will just surface and you will have more than you will even know what to do with it at that point.

IW: Tyler, thank you very much for giving us all this information. It is really an inspiration to listen to you and just really see how much research went into it, but also I am hearing that you had a lot of fun. And this is certainly something that will make any of the authors who are listening want to go ahead and start doing research creating a book for the local area. It sounds like it is really rewarding. Tyler, where can people get in contact with you if they do have questions or want some guidance on how to make a local historical book?

TT: Sure. My website is MarquetteFiction.com and you can see my book *My Marquette* there and my historical novels. My email address is *tyler@marquettefiction.com* and on my website there is also a link there to my blog, so you can leave comments there, and contact me through my blog as well.

IW: Thank you again. This has been a real pleasure having you on this show.

VV: Indeed it has. This has been another podcast edition of Authors Access, where authors get published and published authors get successful. You can learn more about our guest on the Authors Access' website which is *authorsaccess.com*. Authors Access is a joint production of Reader Views Inc. and Loving Healing Press.

IW: And this is Irene from Reader Views saying goodnight.

VV: This is Victor Volkman from Loving Healing Press in Ann Arbor, Michigan, wishing you all a good evening.

Writing Effective Regional Fiction

Understanding Regional Fiction

The first question a person must ask when planning to write regional fiction is "Why will anyone want to read about this region?" That was the question people asked me when I first told them I was writing a series of novels set in my native Upper Michigan. My response was, "Why do we read novels set in Paris or London or Mexico or Australia?" No one thinks twice about reading a novel set in a major city—many of us have never visited New York City, but so many novels have been set there. I know Upper Michigan is just as interesting as New York City, and by focusing on what makes the region unique, I convince my readers to agree with me. Since the regional fiction I write is set in Upper Michigan, I will use examples from my own experiences writing regional fiction, but they are examples that can easily be applied to any locale by any author.

First and foremost, a regional writer must make the region attractive to readers, whether or not they are already familiar with the place. This attraction requires a universally appealing storyline mixed with an emphasis on what makes the setting distinct and interesting. Regional writing is similar in this respect to historical fiction. Historical novelists interest their readers by focusing on the way life has changed since the time they are writing about and what was distinct about that period. Setting a novel in the past is no different than setting a novel in a unique place with its own culture and customs. The past is a strange and fascinating place to us—Isn't it curious that women in 1866 wore hoopskirts? Isn't it bizarre how people wore mourning for two years when a loved one died? Isn't it mind-boggling how they could wear all those clothes during a hot summer just because modesty was more important to them than comfort? What a different world 1866 was compared to the world we know in the early twenty-first century! It is this same focus on the distinctiveness of a specific location that makes regional fiction interesting to the reader.

Regional fiction's origins are really the origins of American literature. Early American writers wanted to distinguish their work from their British counterparts. They differentiated themselves by focusing on what was unique about America. James Fenimore Cooper set his novels in the great forests of New York and brought the Native American element into his novels. Nathaniel Hawthorne used the wildness of the forest as a symbol for human temptations that interfered with the strict Puritan code. Vast and frightening forests had long since ceased to exist in Great Britain, so they were an asset to American literature's originality. The wild animals and Indians that dwelt within these forests were frightening to Cooper and Hawthorne's characters and exciting to their readers. The forest was used to advance the plot and illuminate the motivation of the characters. American and European audiences were fascinated because American literature was unlike anything that had come before it—its regional setting became its distinctive element.

Willa Cather took regional fiction a step further by making the region not only the setting but the protagonist, a character in the story. In my opinion, Cather is the finest American writer of regional fiction—the title of my first novel, *Iron Pioneers*, is a tribute to her masterpiece, *O Pioneers* (1913). In her own words, Cather began writing regional fiction because:

> I had searched for books telling about the beauty of the country I loved; its romance, and heroism, and strength of courage of its people that had been plowed into the very furrows of its soil, and I did not find them. And so I wrote *O Pioneers*!

Finding a Readership for Regional Fiction

Willa Cather's great insight was that if she wanted to read books about the region she lived in, others would as well. Regional writers have a great advantage because their audience is right in their own backyard. And believe me, people want to read about where they live.

I always felt Upper Michigan was someplace special, but I did not realize how special until I moved away. Then I began to miss the long winters, the blankets of snow, the stunning beauty of Lake Superior, the incredible autumn colors—so many priceless aspects of the area. Living away from Upper Michigan for six years allowed me to distance myself from it, to see it afresh and come to appreciate it in new and greater ways; that appreciation helped me to depict Upper Michigan in a manner attractive not only to local readers but also to those not familiar with the area. I felt Upper Michigan, its history and its environmental influence on people, was a significant part of the American story that must be told, just as Cather wanted to record as valuable the life of Nebraska's pioneers. My readers have told me again and again I was right, that they enjoy reading about the place they know and love.

A comment I frequently receive from readers is that now they pay attention to the buildings in Marquette as they drive around the city— they try to pick out the sandstone structures built in the 1800s, and they try to imagine what the city looked like back then. My fiction helps them see the region in a new way, teaching them about the area, and encouraging them to find out more about their own family connections to the place.

I have been especially struck by local people's responses to the cover of my book *The Queen City*. The cover photograph depicts the 1949 Marquette Centennial Parade. It never fails at my book signings that someone will say to me, "That's my grandpa there in the crowd" or "My grandmother was on that float." Senior citizens buy the book because sixty years ago, they stood that day watching the parade on the corner of Washington and Front Streets when they were young and all of life was before them. They are proud they were part of that significant moment in Marquette's history. Their grandchildren buy the book because Grandma is in the photograph, and so they too feel connected to that place and moment in time. Upper Michigan has shaped who they are, and to discover books written about it, written about people like themselves and their forebears, makes them feel their lives are important. These local readers are my core audience, the people who love and revere Upper Michigan as I do.

Marketing regional fiction to readers outside the area is not as easy as selling it to the locals, but it can be just as rewarding. Tourists enjoy

The Marquette Trilogy: Book Two

THE QUEEN CITY

a novel

Tyler R. Tichelaar

The 1949 Centennial Parade has become a touchstone for local families

bringing home books about the places they visit; if they enjoy the books, they tell their neighbors and friends. Furthermore, a host of expatriates from the region are homesick and longing to revisit it through the written word. I get book orders from all over the United States from people who want to read my novels so they can revisit the home of their childhood. They tell their friends—people who have never visited Upper Michigan—about my books, and soon word-of-mouth, the greatest selling point, expands my readership outside Upper Michigan.

People who have never visited Marquette enjoy my novels because they identify with the characters, with the basic themes of love and survival, with the difficult decisions the characters must make—the reasons for why we read and enjoy any good novel. Think of Margaret Mitchell's *Gone With the Wind*—I first saw the film and read the novel when I was only twelve years old. The impression it made upon me is immeasurable—in fact, the first novel I ever wrote, although completely in my head, was a sequel to *Gone With the Wind*. The power of that novel lies in its depiction of a specific region—the Old South—and the distinct way of life in that time and place, a way of life all the more fascinating because it has vanished. The land, especially the plantation of Tara, plays a key role in the story's setting and theme. Early in the novel, Gerald O'Hara emphasizes the land when he talks to Scarlett:

> Land is the only thing in the world that amounts to anything... for 'tis the only thing in this world that lasts, and don't you be forgetting it! 'Tis the only thing worth working for, worth fighting for—worth dying for... And to anyone with a drop of Irish blood in them, the land they live on is like their mother... 'Twill come to you, this love of land. There's no getting away from it, if you're Irish.

This focus on the land makes *Gone With the Wind* regional fiction. That is what the novel largely boils down to. The fight for home, the Confederates' attempt to keep their land and control their property by living the lifestyle they choose. While today we are appalled by slavery, Margaret Mitchell still makes us sympathize with her plantation-owning characters. The novel's themes resonate with readers because they are the very elements we all feel strongly about—the values of home, the threat of your way of life being destroyed, the determination to survive amid all odds, loving someone you cannot have—these elements have made *Gone With the Wind* one of the most successful books of all time. It was twenty years after I read the novel that I finally visited Atlanta, but I did not need to visit the South for Margaret Mitchell's world to come alive for me because she effectively depicted it through her words. Through her characters and descriptions of the events and places, I vicariously lived through the Civil War. Effective regional writing will take a reader to that place, whether it is Atlanta, Nebraska, or Upper Michigan. If a reader can identify with the characters and feel he knows the setting, then any region can be of interest.

Personifying the Region as Protagonist

Willa Cather's greatest contribution to regional fiction was that she altered the region's role from being simply the setting to becoming a character or even the protagonist of the novel. *O Pioneers!* is told in third person through the eyes of Alexandra, but the real hero of the novel—the book's dynamic character—is the land that changes from being dry windswept plains to rich, productive farm country.

The protagonist of regional fiction can be farmland, or equally, a city, county, state, lake, or river. An example of depicting a region as a character occurs in my novel, *Iron Pioneers*. In the following passage, set in Marquette in the winter of 1884, Agnes Whitman has taken her children sledding. She is waiting for them to walk back up the hill when she looks out upon Lake Superior.

> The children were climbing back up the hill, but Agnes still had a couple minutes before they would reach her. She continued to look out at the half-frozen, silent lake, so serene this afternoon; a flood of warm sunlight made its iced surface sparkle like diamonds. Some days that massive lake roared like a bellowing monster; some days it was cruel, as when it had taken Caleb and Madeleine. But the lake was a constant in Agnes's life, something that never failed to revive her spirits when all else came and went. The lake was always there, almost like a family member, someone to quarrel with one day, but ultimately, even if

begrudgingly, to love as a familiar extension of herself, its very water flowing inside her. The lake was a part of her as was the snow, the trees, and these hills she loved so well.

This passage personifies the lake. Agnes realizes she has a relationship with Lake Superior as if it were a family member; it is a love-hate relationship—her siblings have drowned in the lake, but she cannot help but admire its beauty, and its very water feeds her body. My *Marquette Trilogy* covers a century and a half, so the human characters come and go throughout the story; but Lake Superior is a constant throughout the books, a character in itself and one that ties together the novels.

Upper Harbor LS&I Ore Dock in winter
Photo Credit: Sonny Longtine

The Strength is in the Details

Writers always say the best advice about writing is to write what you know. I am from Upper Michigan; I know it well, so I write about it. I could not write as effectively about London or Paris or Florida, all places I've visited but do not know as thoroughly.

A regional writer is already the expert on the area—no one is better qualified to tell the story of that place. But to make the story interesting to people from outside the area, the author needs to determine what is unique and appealing about the region. An effective way to emphasize the region's attributes is to focus on the sensory details, the way the characters experience the region through their senses. In my third novel, *Superior Heritage,* the main character, John Vandelaare, has moved home to Marquette. He wants to write about his native land, and in preparing to do so, he awakens to his own memories and sensory experiences of the region.

> As autumn approached, he became aware again of the Upper Peninsula's special environment. That year, the autumn colors appeared more brilliant than he had remembered them in past years. In the mornings, the smell of rotting leaves gripped his nostrils with a comforting feeling he had not known since childhood's countless autumn walks with [his dog] Dickens. The sunlight sparkling on orange and yellow foliage reawoke a sensitivity to light and color he had long forgotten. Soon, the snow would come with its blinding reflections, its cold, its white wonderland possibilities. One evening, he heard the harmonious honking of the Canadian geese on their southern flight. He looked up into the cold northern sky as darkness spread across it. Quickly he tried to count the V of geese—twenty-six, twenty-seven—he was not quite sure how many, but they were a miracle.

> His senses had reawakened to the voices of birds and the wind, the beauty of leaves and the lake, the smell of snow and an approaching rain shower, the taste of blueberries, the bitter cold biting at his cheeks and fingertips. The singular elements of this land began to mold his imagination, to heighten his senses and his aesthetic appreciation. He had been isolated from Nature's powerful influence while downstate. If he moved away again, he would not have this oneness with his environment that was so essential to his writing; he refused to let himself again forget these little details that made life so splendid. This land had shaped

seven generations of his family, until it had seeped into his being, claiming him as its native son.

**Marquette County Courthouse - film location for *Anatomy of a Murder*
Photo Credit: Sonny Longtine**

This passage demonstrates John's experiences with the region, and vicariously through John's senses, readers themselves sense how it feels to live in Upper Michigan. It is by highlighting what the characters experience through their senses that the region comes alive for the reader.

The power of regional fiction lies in the details, but writers should be cautious because too much attention to detail can be disastrous. I am often asked about writing dialect in regional fiction. Yes, we have a unique dialect in Upper Michigan—the Yooper accent—a mixture of the accents brought by immigrants to Upper Michigan in the nineteenth century from Scandinavia, New England, Canada, and Italy. The accent is similar to that of Northern Minnesota—a slightly exaggerated version of it can be heard in the films *Escanaba in da Moonlight* (2001) and *Fargo* (1996). Dialect and accents are amusing to listen to, but they are not fun to read. Use them sparingly and only to emphasize a point. In *Iron Pioneers*, I have characters who come to the newly founded village of Marquette from Germany and Italy. They speak broken English with an accent, but I only allow them to speak in short sentences. A long string of dialect will slow down the reader who wants to enjoy the story and the plot; readers do not want to translate dialect that is written as if it were almost another language. If you have ever tried to read the Uncle Remus stories, you will know what I mean. They are a perfect example of how not to write dialect. In their day, the stories were commended for capturing slave dialect. Today they are a nearly unreadable curiosity. Leave dialect to the linguists.

Local customs are also something you want to make interesting, but not to the point of boring the reader. It is fine to mention a single unique food from your area, such as the pasty—a meat and potato type pie brought to Upper Michigan by the Cornish miners—but if your book is set in Louisiana, details of a dozen different Cajun foods your readers are not familiar with will not interest them—pick one you want to emphasize and no more. Unless a meal or a food somehow advances the plot or enlightens us about a character, it is unnecessary information.

Do not bore readers with the details of processes. In Upper Michigan, many people are involved in the iron mining industry. In writing my novels, I spent considerable time reading about how iron ore is mined, melted down, made into pellets, transported by railroad to ore boats, and then carried to the steel mills in Pittsburgh or Buffalo. I needed to understand the process of mining and shipping iron ore so my novels were accurate, but my readers do not want to know the temperature required to melt the ore, what the miners' tools looked like, or the dimensions of the ore boats. I only give my readers a taste of a character's experiences working in the iron ore industry; hopefully my readers will be interested enough to find history books to educate them further on the process, but I do not want them distracted from the story by such details.

I provide only the details necessary to develop the character or plot, to make the reader understand the psychological impact of the hard work, the feeling of the heat from a furnace, the dirt and grime of underground mining and why a character may feel frustrated working in the mine, or how working on the ore dock makes him look out over Lake Superior with a longing to travel upon it. The details are less important than how the situation affects the character. My novels have frequently been compared to those of James A. Michener, but the comparison is not always flattering because Michener tended, especially in his later novels, such as *Caribbean*, to fall into writing encyclopedia articles in the middle of his stories. Remember, if details do not advance the plot or develop the character, leave them out. Broad brushstrokes will provide your regional fiction with attractive local color without putting the reader to sleep.

Write What You Know

It's been said a million times, but it's still the best advice any writer can receive: "Write what you know." If you live in the Black Hills of South Dakota, don't write a regional novel set in Florida's Everglades. Write about your hometown, your farm, the place you know the best. You are already an expert on that region—no one else is better qualified than you to tell your story. Draw on your own experiences— go back and remember all the events, memories, feelings you have experienced that are directly related to living in that place. Place your memories and feelings into the minds of your characters—if you can relate to your characters, your readers will relate to them.

Find that quiet but passionate place in your heart that is your personal romance, your own love affair with your land, your town, the lake you live upon—that is the love story that should inspire you and will make your story come alive. Then your readers will feel that the region you write about is home to them, the characters you write about become people your readers half expect to meet in the grocery store or wish they could invite over for dinner.

To allow readers to journey to another place through your words, to make them feel they have actually visited that place—that is the key to writing successful regional fiction.

The preceding article was based on an Authors Access podcast recorded in March 2007. You can find this podcast and many others about regional writing at

http://www.authorsaccess.com/category/genres/regional-books

Donna Winters interview with Tyler Tichelaar

About Donna Winters: Fred and Donna Winters launched the Great Lakes Romances® series in February 1989. Donna adopted Michigan as her home state in 1971 when she moved from a small town outside of Rochester, New York. She began penning novels in 1982 while working full time for an electronics firm in Grand Rapids. Her novels have been published by Thomas Nelson Publishers, Zondervan, Guideposts, and Bigwater Publishing. Learn more about her at **www.GreatLakesRomances.com.**

Donna: In researching local history, would you please list your favorite ways to nail down the data for a writing project?

Tyler: I would suggest you explore and do not overlook all the primary sources available. By primary sources, I mean historical items like newspapers, but also museum collections, city directories, cemetery tombstones, family letters and diaries, oral histories, and of course, the memories of senior citizens in the community. Of course, relying on people's memories causes issues, but so do many printed sources. Newspapers make errors, and relying on a historical article means you're really relying on a secondary source. For nailing down anything, you really need to consult and compare as many sources as possible. For example, I would often find two newspaper articles on a historical event such as the first train coming to Marquette, the town I mostly write history about. One article would say it happened in 1855 and the other that it happened in 1856. In this case, if possible, you should find the newspapers from 1855 or 1856 to confirm. If not, look for a third source and look to see what the sources were for the articles that contradict one another. Too often, people assume someone got a fact right when the person got it wrong, and an error from an article written in 1980 gets repeated in an article in 1995 and 2012 as a result, so you always need to check and double-check and question such details, and it's not just names you need to double-check, but dates, relationships, addresses, and the list goes on.

What was the greatest challenge you faced in writing non-fiction history?

Not being able to pin down facts and having to use my best guesses or be vague about items, or write my way around them. Sadly, I've found lots of details about the period of 1850-1950 in Marquette, but the later twentieth century is not so well documented because it's not thought of as historical yet. Restaurants and businesses that existed in the 1960s or even 1990s that are gone now, no one thought to document for the future, and as a result, much of that information is lost, especially if the owners or family members have passed away also.

What was your greatest challenge in writing fictional history?

For me, the greatest challenge, at least in terms of writing The Marquette Trilogy, was deciding what to leave out because there was so much rich history to choose from. The other challenge was working the history into the plot and imagining how the characters felt about the events they experienced. I decided that every chapter of my trilogy must fulfill three requirements: 1. To depict something historical about the city or period. 2. To develop the characters. 3. To move the plot forward. If an interesting historical detail could not be worked in to include the second and third requirements, I left it out. For example, there was a 1913 trial at the Marquette County Courthouse in which Theodore Roosevelt was involved. It's a great story, but I couldn't figure out how to work that event into the plot, so it is only mentioned in passing. I'm saving it instead to use in more detail in a future novel.

What was the funniest thing that happened to you during your research for a book?

I wish I could tell you the details of that funny moment, but let's just say it involved some information about family members that no one had ever told me, and had remained a family secret for a reason, but that said, the write-up that I found in the newspaper of the event was hilarious. Of course, anything unexpected that I found in my research was fun, and especially anything I found relative to my family's involvement in the community and its history. I love finding out new things about my family and the other people they would have known—that makes facts and history become reality for me. It makes me realize who these people were and how their choices influenced me and how their character traits have been passed down in the family and made me who I am. Whether they made mistakes or they acted nobly with courage, it affected not just them but the generations that followed, and to realize I'm a part of that string of influence is fascinating and fun for me.

Did you run into a lot of fees for using historical photos from museums or other archives?

I wouldn't say "a lot of fees," but yes, you do need to expect to pay fees. Many of my photos in my book My Marquette came from the Marquette Regional History Center, and I believe I paid them $20 for every photo I used from their collection. And that was only to use them in the book. That did not include using them on marketing pieces, my blog, etc. I also got a lot of photos from Superior View, a local photography company that specializes in historical photos. In one case I was refused a photo by a museum—of the Moss Mansion in Montana—I wanted one because that house was the inspiration for a house in my novels—but because my house was fictional, they didn't want the museum associated with it. Fortunately, I already had a photo but was seeking a better quality photo, so I used the one I already had. I also took a lot of my own photos of historical buildings. In those cases, I took exterior photos only. You would need written permission to use interior photos. I was refused to be allowed to take photos at the Marquette Branch Prison, also, but again, I had older photos from when their security was not so high, so the lesson here is always to ask permission before you take photos or use historical photos.

Have you ever had a reader come back to you with, "You got that wrong."?

I'd like to meet the author who hasn't had this happen. Most of the time, an error is not from lack of research, but just a complete lack of knowledge that such could be the case. That's why authors need to do a lot of research. Unfortunately, as I said, a lot of Marquette's more recent history wasn't documented very well, but often it is in living memory, and so people were bound to point out errors to me. I'm glad to say the errors have been very minimal and I did update them in the second edition of My Marquette and I keep a document of corrections as well as updates to be made if I ever come out with a third edition. That's another thing an author has to realize—that your history book will quickly be out of date. Since I wrote My Marquette, three years ago, several of the businesses I mentioned have changed hands or gone out of business, so all those items need to be updated in future editions.

What is your fondest memory, so far, of researching and writing history?

I think what fascinated me most, especially in terms of writing about Marquette, was knowing that my ancestors had lived here and knew and interacted with everyone else whose history I explored. I especially found it fascinating to write about the historical homes in Marquette, owned by the very wealthy, and to realize how closely connected were the families who owned them. I spent a great deal of time trying to unravel family trees. Nearly every family that lived on Ridge and Arch Streets in Marquette was related to every other family by blood or marriage. These people believed in keeping the money in the family.

What's next for you?

I was commissioned last fall by the Marquette Regional History Museum to write a historical play about Will Adams and Norma Ross, who lived in Marquette at the turn of the last century. Adams was "ossified" (a form of paralysis) but he and Norma Ross composed an operetta together, he humming the music and she writing it down. The play is scheduled to be performed at Kaufman Auditorium in Marquette on September 18 and 19 at 7:00 p.m.

I am also branching into writing historical fantasy. I'm currently working on a five volume series, titled The Children of Arthur, which will be set in medieval Europe as well as the modern day and intertwine the legends of many historical and pseudo-historical people such as King Arthur, Melusine, Charlemagne, and Vlad Tepes. Visit my website www.ChildrenofArthur.com for more information and updates. The first volume, Arthur's Legacy, should be out this summer.

And I'm still toying with that Teddy Roosevelt trial....

Thank you, Donna, for the interview. I especially appreciate being interviewed by another fine historical fiction author like yourself.

Books Cited

Cather, Willa. *O Pioneers!* Boston: Houghton Mifflin Co, 1913. Print.

Longtine, Sonny, and Laverne Chappell. *Marquette, Then and Now.* Marquette, MI: North Shore Publications, 1999. Print.

Michener, James A. *Caribbean.* New York, 1989. Print.

Mitchell, Margaret. *Gone with the Wind.* New York: Macmillan, 1936. Print.

Tichelaar, Tyler. *Iron Pioneers: A Novel.* New York, NY: IUniverse, Inc, 2006. Print.

Tichelaar, Tyler. *My Marquette: Explore the Queen City of the North, Its History, People, and Places with Native Son.* Marquette, MI: Marquette Fiction, 2011. Print.

Tichelaar, Tyler. *Narrow Lives: A Novel.* Marquette, MI: Marquette Fiction, 2008. Print.

Tichelaar, Tyler. *The Only Thing That Lasts: A Novel.* Marquette, MI: Marquette Fiction, 2009. Print.

Tichelaar, Tyler. *The Queen City: A Novel.* New York, NY: iUniverse, Inc, 2006. Print.

Tichelaar, Tyler. *Superior Heritage: A Novel.* Marquette, MI: Marquette Fiction, 2007. Print.

Traver, Robert. *Anatomy of a Murder.* New York: St. Martin's Press, 1958. Print.

Watson, Irene, Tyler Tichelaar, and Victor R. Volkman. *Authors Access: 30 Success Secrets for Authors and Publishers.* Ann Arbor, MI: Modern History Press, 2009. Print.

About the Author

Tyler R. Tichelaar is a seventh generation Marquette, Michigan resident. Since age eight he wanted to be a writer. Influenced by stories his grandfather and other family members told him, at age thirteen he wrote his first historical story set in Upper Michigan and at age sixteen, he began writing his first local historical novel.

Tyler has a Ph.D. in Literature from Western Michigan University, and Bachelor and Master's Degrees from Northern Michigan University. Tyler is the regular guest host of Authors Access Internet Radio and the current President of the Upper Peninsula Publishers and Authors Association. He is the owner of his own publishing company, Marquette Fiction, and of Superior Book Promotions, a professional book review, editing, and proofreading service.

Tyler spent thousands of hours researching and writing *The Marquette Trilogy: Iron Pioneers, The Queen City,* and *Superior Heritage,* which tell the story of Marquette, Michigan's history in fiction from 1849-1999.

In 2009, Tyler was awarded the Best Historical Fiction Award in the Reader Views Literary Awards for his novel *Narrow Lives.* He has since gone on to sponsor that award. In 2011, he received the Barb H. Kelly Historic Preservation Award from the Marquette Beautification and Restoration Committee for his local history book *My Marquette: Explore the Queen City of the North*, and he received the Marquette County Arts Award that same year for an "Outstanding Writer."

Tyler's additional regional and historical fiction titles include *The Only Thing That Lasts* and *Spirit of the North: a paranormal romance.*

Tyler has also published the scholarly works *The Gothic Wanderer: From Transgression to Redemption, Gothic Fiction 1794-Present* and *King Arthur's Children: A Study in Fiction and Tradition*, the latter being a precursor to a series of novels about King Arthur he is currently working on.

Tyler lives in Marquette, Michigan where the roar of Lake Superior, mountains of snow, and sandstone architecture inspire his writing. He has many future books in the planning.

You can visit Tyler at his various websites:

www.MarquetteFiction.com

www.GothicWanderer.com www.ChildrenofArthur.com

www.SuperiorBookPromotions.com

Tyler gives the "Sidetracked Book Club" a Marquette history tour

Be Sure to Read All of Tyler R. Tichelaar's Marquette Books

IRON PIONEERS:
THE MARQUETTE TRILOGY: BOOK ONE

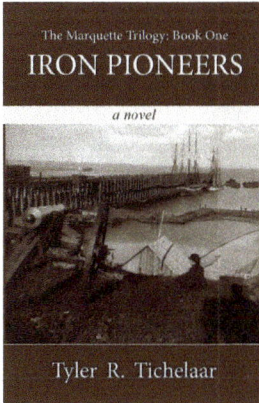

When iron ore is discovered in Michigan's Upper Peninsula in the 1840s, newlyweds Gerald Henning and his beautiful socialite wife Clara travel from Boston to the little village of Marquette on the shores of Lake Superior. They and their companions, Irish and German immigrants, French Canadians, and fellow New Englanders face blizzards and near starvation, devastating fires and financial hardships. Yet these iron pioneers persevere until their wilderness village becomes integral to the Union cause in the Civil War and then a prosperous modern city. Meticulously researched, warmly written, and spanning half a century, *Iron Pioneers* is a testament to the spirit that forged America.

THE QUEEN CITY:
THE MARQUETTE TRILOGY: BOOK TWO

During the first half of the twentieth century, Marquette grows into the Queen City of the North. Here is the tale of a small town undergoing change as its horses are replaced by streetcars and automobiles, and its pioneers are replaced by new generations who prosper despite two World Wars and the Great Depression. Margaret Dalrymple finds her Scottish prince, though he is neither Scottish nor a prince. Molly Bergmann becomes an inspiration to her grandchildren. Jacob Whitman's children engage in a family feud. The Queen City's residents marry, divorce, have children, die, break their hearts, go to war, gossip, blackmail, raise families, move away, and then return to Marquette. And always, always they are in love with the haunting land that is their home.

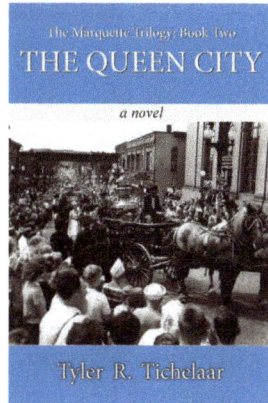

SUPERIOR HERITAGE
THE MARQUETTE TRILOGY: BOOK THREE

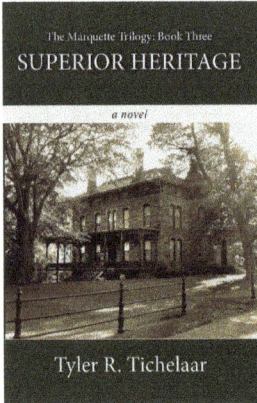

The Marquette Trilogy comes to a satisfying conclusion as it brings together characters and plots from the earlier novels and culminates with Marquette's sesquicentennial celebrations in 1999. What happened to Madeleine Henning is finally revealed as secrets from the past shed light upon the present. Marquette's residents struggle with a difficult local economy, yet remain optimistic for the future. The novel's main character, John Vandelaare, is descended from all the early Marquette families in *Iron Pioneers* and *The Queen City*. While he cherishes his family's past, he questions whether he should remain in his hometown. Then an event happens that will change his life forever.

NARROW LIVES
RETURN TO MARQUETTE...

Narrow Lives is the story of those whose lives were affected by Lysander Blackmore, the sinister banker first introduced to readers in *The Queen City*. It is a novel that stands alone, yet readers of *The Marquette Trilogy* will be reacquainted with some familiar characters. Written as a collection of connected short stories, each told in first person by a different character, *Narrow Lives* depicts the influence one person has, even in death, upon others, and it explores the prisons of grief, loneliness, and fear self-created when people doubt their own worthiness.

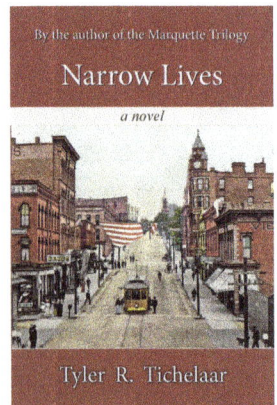

THE ONLY THING THAT LASTS

The story of Robert O'Neill, the famous novelist introduced in *The Marquette Trilogy*. As a young boy during World War I, Robert is forced to leave his South Carolina home to live in Marquette with his grandmother and aunt. He finds there a cold climate, but many warmhearted friends. An old-fashioned story that follows Robert's growth from childhood to successful writer and husband, the novel is written as Robert O'Neill's autobiography, his final gift to Marquette by memorializing the town of his youth.

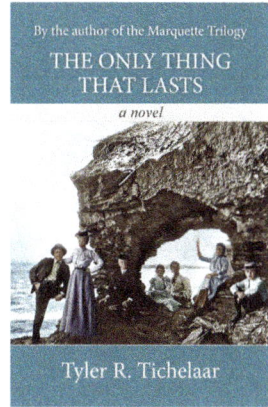

MY MARQUETTE:
EXPLORE THE QUEEN CITY OF THE NORTH
—ITS HISTORY, PEOPLE, AND PLACES

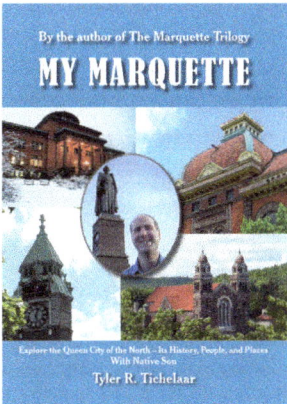

My Marquette is the result of its author's lifelong love affair with his hometown. Join Tyler R. Tichelaar, seventh generation Marquette resident and author of *The Marquette Trilogy*, as he takes you on a tour of the history, people, and places of Marquette. Stories of the past and present, both true and fictional, will leave you understanding why Marquette really is "The Queen City of the North." Along the way, Tyler will describe his own experiences growing up in Marquette, recall family and friends he knew, and give away secrets about the people behind the characters in his novels. *My Marquette* offers a rare insight into an author's creation of fiction and a refreshing view of a city's history and relevance to today. Reading *My Marquette* is equal to being given a personal tour by someone who knows Marquette intimately.

For more information on Tyler's Marquette Books, visit:

www.MarquetteFiction.com

Tyler R. Tichelaar Embarks Into Gothic Fiction

SPIRIT OF THE NORTH
A Paranormal Romance

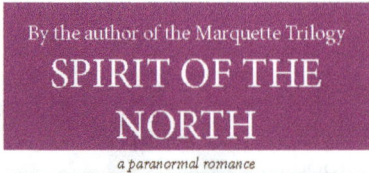

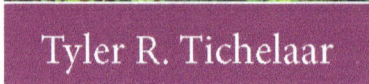

By the author of the Marquette Trilogy

SPIRIT OF THE NORTH

a paranormal romance

Tyler R. Tichelaar

In 1873, orphaned sisters Barbara and Adele Traugott travel to Upper Michigan to live with their uncle, only to find he is deceased. Penniless, they are forced to spend the long, fierce winter alone in their uncle's remote wilderness cabin. Frightened yet determined, the sisters face blizzards and near starvation to survive. Amid their difficulties, they find love and heartache—and then, a ghostly encounter and the coming of spring lead them to discovering the true miracle of their being.

Influenced by the Gothic tradition, Tichelaar weaves stories within stories, including ghost stories and a tale of Paul Bunyan, all containing supernatural elements. And among them is the tale of Annabella Stonegate, a minor character in some of Tichelaar's previous novels, whose story is told in full here. "Annabella was a ghost in a story I wrote in middle school," says Tichelaar, "she has haunted me for more than a quarter of a century, insisting I tell her full story. I think I have finally satisfied her insistence."

For more information, visit **www.MarquetteFiction.com**

NOTES:

www.ingramcontent.com/pod-product-compliance
Lightning Source LLC
Chambersburg PA
CBHW071754020426
42331CB00008B/2308